My Beautiful Fire

Katelyn Jade Guynup

BookLeaf
Publishing

Presentation by *BookLeaf Publishing*

Web: www.bookleafpub.com

E-mail: info@bookleafpub.com

ISBN: 9789395255271

First edition 2022

DEDICATION

To the clever fox that got away you hold a very special in my heart. I hope you come to see that one day . The jack o lantern smile that could light up a whole room . The one who cracked me wide open and made me start working on myself . I don't know how I could ever thank you . I know in some ways I broke your heart but I promise I didn't mean to . I'll miss you and I hope one day you see this . You made me believe in myself .

To the cat thank you for being there during those late night phone calls and holding my hand when I needed it the most . I don't know where I would be without you some days . Honestly to call you a best friend is an honor in itself . I'm glad to have a friend like you to break down walls with .

My day one thank you for being there through 15 years of friendship . You've seen my high and lows plus everything in between . You've had my back when every the cards were stacked against me . I love you the most.

Invasion

I let you invade me .
I let you crawl between my skin.
Each touch felt like an attack and my body full
of sin.

I didn't want you there but I always said yes.
I thought avoiding the argument was for the
best.
My body and mind were never at rest.
You always said I wish you the best.
I lost pieces of myself when I was with you I
never shined anymore because I couldn't take
away from your light .
The walls around me felt to close and very tight.
In my heart and head I knew this wasn't right .

You tried to snuff me out like I was a piece of
shit on your shoe. I am thankful I got away from
you .

You could no longer hurt me but the damage you
did would stick.

Skeletons in the closet

I keep some skeletons in my closet.
I'll never throw away the key because deep
down they're apart of me.
In the darkness they held the light so I could see
.

I lost the soul for the girl inside of me.
I never knew who she was but they sure did
instead of suffocating me they tried to help me
win.
The lines drawn in the sand were very thin.
My bones once fragile and cracked beneath the
skin .
I'm starting to grow and become the person
within .

Icarus

3

Icarus flew to close to the sun
His wings melted off so all he could do was run
I offered to mend his wings so he could fly but a
little piece of me would soon die
I told him I didn't love him that was a lie.
As I kiss and reach for the stars that paint the
night sky
I think of you the man who could fly .
Who could see the beauty within these eyes .

Close the door

Close the door but don't throw away the key.

Do you even see me ?
Not perfect or pretty but flawed and bruised .

Imperfections at their finest an artist painting
their muse.

Colors displayed across a canvas with different
shades of violets and blues.

You paint the picture the way you see.

The masterpiece made from
Mistakes of you and me.

Vulnerable

5

I fell in love with the most vulnerable parts of
you .

Some had sharp edges and thorns but that didn't
scare me away . I tried my best to hold on and
stay . It was me who ran away .

Your eyes the crashing waves of green and blue
they reminded me so much of the sea .

I adored you couldn't you see .
The violent blues and misty greens are what I
lived for when I lost you at sea.

Icarus and the Flame

We dance around the flames trying not to burned
.

I wonder what we could've learned .
Did we get what we deserved ?
We played to close to fire again .
Hearts broken that I don't know if we'll ever
mend .
Please don't tell me this is the end because I
believed in me and you .
The fire inside doesn't think this story is through
.

I've torn out pages and started my book over
brand new .
I hope someday the story begins with me and
you .
I've learned the fire you once saw was buried
deep inside of me .
I was just blinded and couldn't see.
You held my hand even though I burned yours
so many times .
I wish I could take it all back and try .

Wishbone

7

My bones are full of wishes for me and you .
I guess I gotta sit and see this on through.
I have a feeling what once was broken can be new.
You were the missing puzzle piece I just didn't have a clue .

My bones wish for you
In the very worst way
I know I begged and pleaded for you to stay .
Maybe we had to go our separate ways in order to grow.
Our love story could not be brought or sold.
So many secrets and stories left untold.

Falling Star

8

They say to catch a falling star and put it in your
pocket save it for a rainy day .

What if the stars shatter like glass and these
webs we call life lines don't last ?

What's if I can't put you in the past we go
through the motions but time moves to fast .

I wasn't perfect but neither were you .
Are we like a bouquet of dead roses that will
never see the light to bloom.

Fragile

You have all these precious things that fill your
home but you continue to put up walls made of
stone .

Every wall lined in silver and gold but why is it
we feel so alone .

Hollow and cold a heart made from fragments of
glass .

You whisper in my ear like the devil on back
will this even last ?

Wishes fall upon deaf ears .
Do we watch the stars shatter and live in fear .
The galaxies will swallow use whole my dear.
We'll ask ourselves at the end did it really matter
while we sit down and watch our whole
foundation shatter.

Clever Little Fox

Clever little fox you hide your heart away.
I wonder if you'll stay ?
Can you come out and play another day ?

We can paint the sky with stars and galaxies that
move you .
I promise I won't let them lose you .

Maybe I told you that I loved you to soon .
I remember those crisp fall afternoons .

The flowers are weak now and won't bloom.
I think they miss you I know I do .

I think our time stopped to soon .

Can we go back to those crisp fall afternoons ?

Where the rabbit would play and the fox would
stay .

I could lay in your arms everyday and paint our
future bright but that's looking a little far out of
sight .

I think I had to lose the most beautiful parts of
you to find myself . I think I loved your more
than anyone else .

For now I'll put this old heart on the shelf and
hope one day you'll come back to me .

Homesick

I've been homesick for awhile for the people
who chew me up and spit me out .

I've been dealing with years of self doubt .
I was never enough for you .
I felt like chewing gum on a broken down pair
of shoes .

For the ghost running across the kitchen floor .
The candle once lit hoping for more .
The little girl I once adored let her light fade out
.

The twinkle she once had laced with poison and
self doubt .

I've been homesick for awhile for the noise that
filled the empty places of my heart .

I knew what you promised me was a lie from the
start.

Your conniving smile a work of art .
The emotional scars you left would take me time
to pull apart.

The good things presented to me would fall
apart .
I would have to go back to the very start and
burn down the house to bare bones .
I would have to start to rebuild from years that
held my soul .
I will not miss you I tell myself because these
secrets I keep a poison the well.

I've met beautiful people I am to afraid to touch
because you've tainted my luck .

You took some of the most beautiful parts of me
and buried them in the ground .
The flowers don't grow there and the birds make
no sound .

I hope someday the once beautiful parts of me
can be found .

Little girl

I never knew her through the waves of depression.

I never saw who she could be the picture was always blurry and I couldn't see.

How could he ever understand me .

I threw up walls over and over again to keep my heart safe .

I felt lonely and out of place that was my biggest mistake.

I would try and muster a smile but some days they were fake.

I never understood the give and take.

I threw my walls up with you and never let you in .

I'm sorry about that and the fact I put your heart in a tail spin .

I wish I could've told you how I felt .

I wish I didn't hide my secrets all to well.

The demons that eat me alive while they disguise their smiles as gentle lullabies.

I wish I didn't say I was fine .

The secrets written on my body and behind my eyes .

I wish I told you the truth instead of choosing to lie.

My demons slowly ate me alive taking away the best parts of me .

I always said I was fine .

I could tell that you saw behind my eyes that things were slowly crumbling beneath my skin.

You tried to save me from myself .

I have nobody else to blame when I threw your heart away.

The Knight

Break down all the skin and bones .

I promise darling your not alone.

The ground is gonna be hard and full of gravel
and stone .

I promise you won't walk this alone .

The fears you once had let me carry them
The doubt I see it in your eyes I promise darling
they're all lies .

The mask you wear I see through your disguise .

I see the cracks within your smile and the pain
behind your eyes .

I promise I won't tell you any lie.

I'll guide you to the place I call paradise .

Darling you can rest I promise I'll defend you
when put to the test.

I know these old war wounds don't look the best
but my heart is full of gold that I can attest .

I never thought I could put down this sword and
armor till I met you .

Any promise I make know I gotta see it through
it's all because you.

I miss you and the parts you cracked wide open
so many words left unspoken .

Here's to hoping .

First

Your pictures didn't do you justice or the way you held my hand .

I would've cherished it a little bit more if I didn't feel like time was quick sand .

I wish you would understand .

The way you smiled it made me want to stay for awhile but all I could do was run .

I'm sorry I was Icarus I flew to close to the sun .

I felt like I didn't deserve the happiness with all the secrets I would keep .

The little demons would fester and not let me sleep .

The little voices said you would leave and that I would truly never give you the chance .

It was you I wanted to believe and how you saw me .

I wish I could see me that way .

I'm growing a little into her day by day .

The lights on but nobody's home

Will you light my way home even if it's dark outside ?

Will you keep me safe inside ?

Will you always lay by my side and never let the fire die .

You told me little lies while our finger tips traced the night sky .

A part of me died inside when you broke my heart that July .

You were my home and the reasons why the spaces never felt empty .

Those ghost blue eyes were a private entry .

I loved you like no other even though you walked away for another .

I wish

People tell me their worth the investment .

We build tiny homes and light a fire along the way .

We wish and hope someone will stay but we gradually push each other away .

Do I stand my ground or walk away ?

I'm trying to figure out how to communicate with you till this very day .

Do I let my secrets pour over out of this cup or do I place my bet on the rabbits luck .

Honestly there are some days I want to scream fuck but I hold my composure .

I tell the women inside of me I wish you luck.

It's gonna be painful and messy but who knows where this will lead .

The lies of romance and love blasted on a tv
screen .

Love is messy and sometimes unkind but it all
lies behind these beautiful blue green eyes .

I thought I could bury you and put you in the
past but my heart said hold up not to fast .

There was something special about you that I
wanted to last but I got ahead of myself and
moved to fast .

I wish I could take back all the things I said
instead of laying here alone in this bed .

I wish I listened when you told me to get help .

I wish I told you all the things that I ever felt .

I wish I could have Saturday mornings back
with a fluffy fox bear retriever .

I wish so much I may start to believe in her .

The Moth

I feel like I keep searching in the darkness for
some kind of light .

I hold my breath tight .

I wonder if this is worth the fight.

Who was wrong and who was right ?

My fist clench into my skin very tight .

The wings of the moth burn away very bright .

The light that flickers goes in and out .

My mind automatically shifts to self doubt.

Will I ever come out of this alive or will I let
another piece of me die .

I try to tell myself I will strive amongst the
thorns in garden I created .

I won't let another part of me be sedated .

The Winter House

I sometimes wish I wasn't your rabbit .
I sometimes wish I could come up for air.
I wish sometimes I didn't care.

Forever trapped in those blue eyes and that
loving stare I wouldn't dare .

Trapped inside this house I created bones laid
naked and bare what we had was rare .
The windows are open .
The winter cold is setting in .
Words left unspoken my skin stands on needles
and pins.

I wish I could see the tragic events that would
devour me from within .

I wish I let you help but I couldn't even save
myself.

Keep me close

25

Keep me close
Keep me safe

I know often feelings are misplaced
I'll own up to my mistakes .
I can't run and hide from this place .
I can't erase what could've been or what should
be .
The future is not mine to see .
It's the little things you promised me I try to
believe .
I'll hold onto hope while fighting for me .

My Beautiful Fire

My beautiful fire don't you see what you mean
to me .

You can burn down cities and build houses in
between .

Can't you see what you mean to me .

The gorgeous flames played out like a painting
on a fresh canvas .

Nobody can touch your light that shines oh so
bright .

You know sometimes that your not right .

You love to hard or to little .
The devil on your shoulder playing his fiddle .

The little red man will sell you his riddles
of intrusive thoughts and self doubt .

Just please remember what your about .

Remember that your beautiful and will be seen .

Remember who you are and come back to me.

I believe

I believe in you even when no one else will see
you through.

I'll hold you through the laughter and tears.

My beautiful fire I hold you oh so close and oh
so dear love you life without fear .

Halloween

The jack o lantern smile that cracked me wide open.

The leaves on the ground stepped on and broken
.

The colors played out like vibrant shades yellow and red .

The fall were everything that once bloomed is now dead .

So many words left unsaid .

I wish I could hold your hand instead.

The ghost that haunt the house I once lived in now have become dear friends .

I've learned from my mistakes and won't repeat them again.

The skeletons that always greeted me at the door I once hated now I adore.

I learned a lesson from them that I can't live in
the past .

I know time heals all wounds but it won't be to
fast .

I have so much I want to say but don't know
how to .

I think my mind sometimes won't allow me to.

Th floor boards creak beneath my feet where all
the little mice would once sleep.

I know I allowed myself to sink to deep.

I need to open the windows and let the crisp
morning air through .
I know some days it will remind me of you.